WOODY GUTHRIE

So Long, It's Been Good to Kno

I'm A-Goin' Back to th' Farm

oklah

I Ain't Got No Home

this land is your land

hard tra

ballad of isaac

"Deportee" ("Plane Wreck at Los Gatos")

Sl

grand coulee dam

Wake

Dust Bowl Refugee

this train is bou

Talking Hitler's Head off Blues

pastures of p

Roll On Columbia

Jackhamm

Dust Pneumonia Blues

Union Mai

dust storm disaster

dust can'

The Ballad of Pretty Boy Floyd

Curly-Headed Baby

Do Re Mi

WOODY GUTHRIE

America's

Folksinger

Karen Mueller Coombs

Carolrhoda Books, Inc./Minneapolis

Note to Reader
Woody Guthrie's writing style varied from folksy to
elegant. Sometimes his grammar, spelling, and
punctuation were perfect; other times they were
filled with errors. Quotations included in this book
reproduce Woody's words exactly as he wrote them,
mistakes and all.

*For my brothers, Roger and Craig, who, like Woody, follow their own roads and
sing their own songs.*

Acknowledgments
For their constant support and wise comments as the book grew from idea to
fruition, I thank my writers' group. My gratitude also to Harold Leventhal of
the Woody Guthrie Foundation for his guidance and encouragement; to my
editor, Margaret Goldstein, for her enthusiasm and her skill at shepherding
the manuscript through the editing process; and to my patient husband, Jon,
and my children, Cameron and Carlin.

Carolrhoda Books, Inc.
A division of Lerner Publishing Group
241 First Avenue North
Minneapolis, MN 55401 U.S.A.

Website address: www.lernerbooks.com

Library of Congress Cataloging-in-Publication Data

Coombs, Karen Mueller, 1947–
    Woody Guthrie : America's folksinger / by Karen Mueller Coombs.
       p.   cm. — (Trailblazer biography)
Includes bibliographical references and index.
    ISBN: 1-57505-464-7 (lib. bdg. : alk. paper)
    1. Guthrie, Woody 1912–1967—Juvenile literature. 2. Folk singers—
United States—Biography—Juvenile literature. [1. Guthrie, Woody
1912–1967. 2. Singers. 3. Folk music.] I. Title. II. Series.
ML3930.G88 C66 2002
782.42162'13'0092—dc21   00-010087

Manufactured in the United States of America
1 2 3 4 5 6 – JR – 07 06 05 04 03 02

Contents

Woody Guthrie lives on through his classic American folk songs.

"This Land Is Your Land"

A crowd of more than one thousand filled Pythian Hall in New York on March 17, 1956. The people had come to honor Woody Guthrie, one of the nation's most famous folksingers and songwriters. Onstage, Woody's old friends and companions read his words and sang his songs—songs such as "So Long, It's Been Good to Know Yuh," "Roll On, Columbia," and "This Train Is Bound for Glory."

For a brief two decades, Woody Guthrie wrote and sang of his feelings about the United States. In that short time span, he also composed journals, letters, essays, poems, newspaper columns, radio shows, and more than one thousand songs: love songs, work songs, hobo songs, outlaw ballads. He wrote about disasters, the simple joys of childhood, the working man's struggle, the black man's misery, the fight against Adolf Hitler, and the beauty he saw around him. Mainly, he wrote songs of hope, because Woody Guthrie believed that given the right song, downtrodden and discouraged people everywhere could rise up singing.

The Pythian Hall concert closed with the entire cast singing `This Land Is Your Land.` Suddenly, the

Woody rises from his balcony seat in Pythian Hall during a tribute to his life's work on March 17, 1956.

spotlight swung to the darkened balcony. It shone on a spidery, bushy-haired man, who struggled awkwardly to rise, then raised a clenched fist to greet the audience.

Recognizing Woody, the crowd surged to its feet, cheering. The song ended. Woody's friend and fellow folksinger Pete Seeger—tears streaming down his cheeks—began the first verse again. The audience joined in, filling the hall with Woody's most famous song, telling him they would carry his music across the land and into the future.

Clara holds baby Woody. Their brother Roy is on the right.

1

"Oklahoma Hills"

The clop of the horse's hooves rang on the hard clay long before the rider came into view. Six-year-old Woody Guthrie sprinted down Ninth Street toward the sound, his wild curls bouncing. His father saw him coming, reached down, and scooped the scrawny boy onto the saddle in front of him. Then Charley Guthrie began one of the silly word games he and Woody loved:

"Where've you been, my curly head?"
"I been a playin' in the big high weeds."
"Who did you play with? What did you play?"
"Played bows and arrows and war all day."
"Did you have any fuss? Did you have any fights?"
"One big fuss, an' two little fights."

From the beginning, Woody Guthrie had rhythm and music in his life.

Woodrow Wilson Guthrie, named after the twenty-eighth president of the United States, was born on July 14, 1912, in Okemah, Oklahoma. He was the third of Charley and Nora Guthrie's five children.

Woody's father was a dreamer and a schemer who held many jobs over the years, including clerk, bookkeeper, and assistant postmaster. He ran for political office several times and was elected county clerk twice. Before Woody was born, Charley Guthrie had earned enough money buying and selling land to build his family a six-room house with a porch wrapped around three sides.

Charley liked spending the money he earned, and he thought nothing could go wrong. So when the house

Woody was born in this house in Okemah, Oklahoma, on July 14, 1912.

Woody's parents, Charley and Nora Guthrie, 1917

burned down just a month after the family moved in, Charley didn't have enough fire insurance and had no money saved. A few possessions were rescued, but the family was left nearly penniless.

A few years after Woody came along, the family moved to a dreary, dank stone house built into the side of a hill. Woody's older sister, Clara, and his older brother, Roy, hated the house. So did his mother. But Woody, not yet school-age, liked the back porch that clung to the second floor. From the porch of the stone house, Woody could look down over the sun-fried, wind-scoured town of Okemah. He watched the cotton wagons, tipsy with their high white loads, creak into the cotton mill. He saw the smoke-belching steam engines chug away from the railroad station.

But there was something Woody didn't like about the stone house. His early years had been filled with the sounds of his mother playing piano and singing lullabies, nonsense songs, hymns, and ballads. Now, perhaps because she hated the stone house, Nora didn't sing as much. And sometimes she acted sad, mixed up, and angry.

World War I began in Europe in 1914. Although the United States didn't enter the war right away, American food crops were important to the war effort. Farmland became more valuable and began to change hands. Charley Guthrie bought more land and soon owned thirty farms outside Okemah. On one, he raised prize cattle, hogs, and hunting dogs. In 1915 he was elected justice of the peace, a low-level political job.

Around 1918 Charley bought a house on Okemah's North Ninth Street. That year, Woody's brother George was born. After work, Charley would greet the children with word games and songs that made Woody's "ears stand away out and wiggle for more."

Woody's father taught the children to ride horses, but Woody fell off a horse and broke his right elbow in three places. After the arm was set, he promptly fell out of a tree and jarred the arm, so it didn't heal properly. For the rest of his life, Woody had a crooked right forearm.

After the move to the house on Ninth Street, Woody's mother, Nora, seemed fine for a while. But soon she began reminding Woody of the days in the stone house. Only thirty-one years old, she became forgetful. She left chores half finished and dressed her children in ragged, dirty clothes. Sometimes she wandered around town for no reason. But what frightened and worried Woody the

Nora's strange behavior sometimes frightened her children.

most was Nora's temper. She lost it often, especially with Woody's big sister, Clara.

Woody, eight years younger, adored his sister. Clara, he said, danced to school and sang her way home. Her long curls brushed his face when she wrestled him across the floor.

One day in May 1919, when Woody was nearly seven, Nora kept Clara home from school to do some housework. Clara wanted to go to school to take an important exam, and she argued with her mother. Exactly what happened next isn't known. One story says that Clara was cleaning the stove and spilled kerosene on her dress. Later, when the fire wouldn't burn properly, she opened

Woody adored his big sister, Clara (pictured here with Roy).

the stove door to fix it. Fresh air poured into the stove. The flames flared up, setting Clara's dress on fire.

The other explanation, suggested by Clara herself right after the fire, is sadder. Clara, angry with her mother, knew Nora had been terrified of fire since their house had burned down years earlier. Clara decided to get even. She dribbled some kerosene on her dress and—intending only to scare her mother—lit a match. The dress exploded in flames.

However the accident began, Clara ran screaming from the house. A neighbor with a blanket helped smother the blaze. But Clara was horribly burned from her neck to her knees. Her nerve endings were destroyed, so she felt no pain.

Afterward, Clara lay in bed, covered in bandages, cheerfully chatting with grieving friends and family. She even granted an interview with the local newspaper. Clara told Woody that she would soon be up singing and dancing again. Then she made him promise that he would never cry—crying only made people feel bad. Soon after, Clara died.

Woody's grieving father seemed to age overnight. Woody's mother spoke of nothing but her dead daughter. Rumors flew around town. Some people, remembering the house fire years before, claimed that Nora had set the first fire and perhaps had even had a hand in this new one.

To escape the busy tongues and staring eyes, the family moved to one of Charley's farms outside town. But their misery followed them. Nora sat around the house sobbing and crying out that she wanted to die. Sometimes her face twitched, and she curled her lips and showed her teeth. Spit ran from her mouth, and her arms would swing and jerk. These were signals that she was turning into that "other" person—the one who screamed and fell writhing on the floor, the one who didn't care how sloppy or awful she looked.

At night Woody dreamed that his mother was like other mothers and that he would wake to see her smiling as she fixed his breakfast or mended his clothes. Instead, he and his brother Roy would get up to the same terrible mess and do what they could to make life better.

Woody *(left)*, Charley *(seated center)*, and George *(right)*, in about 1926. Nora stands behind them.

2

"I Ain't Got No Home"

In the 1920s, people swarmed into Okemah. Oil had been discovered near the town, and it was valuable. Some men came looking for work on the oil rigs. Others set up businesses to sell supplies to the rigs and the workers. Within months, the town's population rose from two thousand to ten thousand.

Woody's father knew the local land and the people. He seemed poised to make a fortune selling land to the oil seekers. But Clara's death had taken the drive out of Charley Guthrie. Although he tried to compete with high-powered land dealers who flocked into town, he no longer had the energy.

By 1923 the Guthries were broke again. And there was a new mouth to feed. Mary Josephine had been born in February 1922. In July 1923, the family moved to a shack in Oklahoma City. Every able family member took a job. Charley, unable to find steady work, earned a dollar's worth of food a day delivering groceries. Roy pumped gas. Woody, now eleven, delivered milk. It was a sad, hopeless time.

The Guthries staggered back to Okemah the following summer and set up house in a rotting, abandoned shack. The oil boom was over, taking with it the new businesses and people, leaving only the cotton and pecan farmers and the newly paved streets. Charley eventually got a job issuing car licenses at fifty cents each. In pain from arthritis, he began to drink often.

Nora hated the shack. Feeling more miserable, dizzy, and uncoordinated than ever, she continued her strange behavior. She pitched furniture and food into the yard. She escaped to the local movie theater nearly every day. There, she could sit unnoticed in the dark and watch the screen antics of silent-film star Charlie Chaplin, the one person who still made her laugh. Local doctors couldn't explain her condition. The townspeople thought she was insane.

Twelve-year-old Woody started spending more time away from home, more time playing hooky. He drifted around the fringes of town, scavenging junk in a burlap bag, "digging like a mole into everybody's trash heaps to see if I couldn't make a little something out of nothing."

At the barbershop, he soaked up local stories and tall tales and listened to the shoeshine boy make his

Woody posed with his Okemah High School classmates during the
1926–1927 school year. He sits in the front row, fifth from left.

harmonica sound like a lonesome train. Play it again,
Woody pestered. And again. Soon Woody had his own
harmonica and was playing old songs and ballads he had
learned from his mother—"Barbara Allen," "Gypsy
Davy," "Sailor's Plea"—all over town.

At school, kids teased Woody for being small, for his
sharp Adam's apple and his unruly curls, for being shabby
and poor. Woody pretended not to care. He became the
class clown—playing the harmonica, dancing jigs, and
drawing funny cartoons. When he didn't feel like going
to school, Woody hid out in an abandoned tin shack.

The children were no longer safe with their mother.
One day, when eight-year-old George refused to bathe in
a tub of freezing water, Nora chased him with a knife.
Another time, she let three-year-old Mary Jo wander out
of a movie theater and into the street. Finally, in 1926,

Woody's father sent Mary Jo and George to their aunt's home in Texas. Woody hardly ever went home. He slept on benches around town. His harmonica playing earned him meals at the back doors of local cafés.

In April 1927, Charley lost his job issuing licenses. Then, one evening in June, he ran screaming from the house, his clothes on fire. The badly burned Charley refused to say what had happened, but the *Okfuskee County News* reported that he had been doused by kerosene. A rumor spread that Nora had thrown a burning lamp on Charley. The next day, doctors took Woody's mother to the state hospital for the mentally ill in Norman, Oklahoma. Woody, who had been visiting his grandmother when his father was burned, never got to say good-bye.

As soon as he felt well enough to travel, Woody's father followed George and Mary Jo to Texas, leaving Roy and Woody to fend for themselves. Roy, age twenty-one, earned enough money as a grocery clerk to pay for his own room and board. Woody, fifteen, was farmed out to different families around town, but soon he fled to his tin shack. He no longer went to school.

When he was hungry, it was easy to steal some milk and beg some bread. If he didn't feel like stealing or begging, he went downtown, set out his cap, played his harmonica, and danced. Soon the cap would be full of coins, and Woody full of the pleasure that comes from setting toes to tapping and hands to clapping.

Other kids used Woody's shack as a hangout. There they enjoyed slingshot fights and bow-and-arrow wars. Most were easygoing youngsters who didn't judge

Woody for being poor but simply accepted him the way he was. One of them was Casper Moore. His father, Tom Moore, was a friend of Woody's father.

When winter arrived, rain oozed into the shack. Casper Moore begged his parents to take Woody in, and they agreed. Woody tried to fit into the Moore family. He even went back to school, where he made little effort but received average grades. He got his best marks in typing and geography. He worked on the school newspaper and as the joke editor of the yearbook. He played harmonica and danced to raise money for school events. When he earned sixty dollars entertaining at a Rotary Club meeting, Woody bought two new shirts, then gave away the rest of the money.

Woody lived with the Moores for a year, a year filled with family life—and music. After dinner, Tom Moore would take out his fiddle, and the family would sing hymns and ballads until bedtime. Woody played harmonica or sang harmony—blending his voice with the sounds of the lead singer. He often made up new, witty lyrics as they were singing.

Late in 1928, the Moores decided to move to Arizona. Before they left, they drove Woody sixty miles to the hospital in Norman to visit his mother for the first time. By then, Nora Guthrie was a shaking, fidgeting shell of a woman. She didn't recognize her sixteen-year-old son. She had Huntington's chorea, a disease of the nervous system, the doctors told Woody. She could not be cured.

That was the last time Woody saw his mother. Despite his promise to his dying sister that he would never cry, he wept all the way home to Okemah.

When hard times hit the United States in 1929, many Americans were forced to move to ramshackle camps. Here, a homeless man tastes stew in a makeshift kitchen.

3

"Goin' Down the Road"

After the Moores left Okemah, there was nothing and no one to hold Woody there. Some friends had moved to the Gulf of Mexico at the Texas coast. Woody decided to visit them. Early in the summer of 1929, he started hitch-hiking south.

If he was near a town at sundown, Woody would scout out hobo camps at the edge of railroad yards. There, he would be welcome to share a pot of bubbling stew. Most of the men he met in the camps were unemployed labor-ers or migrant farmworkers, following the ripening crops across the country. All had tales to tell and songs to share.

When he reached the Gulf of Mexico, Woody sniffed the salty tang of seawater for the first time. He found his friends, who put him to work on their farm. Never fond of hard labor, Woody quickly escaped and headed home. Back in Okemah, he found a letter from his father. Now recovered from his burns, Charley had moved to Pampa, a town in northwestern Texas. He asked Woody to join him there and help him run a rooming house.

Like Okemah a few years earlier, Pampa was an oil boomtown. On the lower level of Charley's seedy, two-story rooming house, tired oil workers rented cots for eight-hour stretches at twenty-five cents each. Seventeen-year-old Woody drank in the talk of the oil workers as he helped his father change linens and collect money. He soon had a job running the soda fountain at a drugstore for three dollars a day. In the 1920s and early 1930s, selling liquor was illegal in the United States. Even so, if a customer plunked $1.50 on the counter, Woody would deliver a two-ounce bottle of "moonshine," usually corn whiskey.

In his spare time, Woody decorated the drugstore windows and the mirror behind the fountain with cartoons and signs. Outside, on the bricks above the front window, he painted "Harris Drug," signing "Woody" next to the name. The sign remained on the building for forty-eight years.

One day Woody found a shabby guitar in the store. He began picking out the old songs his mother had taught him. His Uncle Jeff—his father's younger half brother and the best country fiddler in the panhandle—taught him to play chords.

Plucking the guitar and selling moonshine didn't show the kind of drive that Charley wanted to see in his nearly grown son. Impressed by Woody's drawings, Charley enrolled him in a home-study course in cartooning. Charley also began nudging Woody to return to high school for his diploma. Woody didn't take kindly to nudging, but he finally agreed to go back to school. It was there that he met Matt Jennings.

Matt—tall, red-haired, and freckle-faced—was also an outsider from a poor family. Together the boys swam, shot rats at the town dump, and attended wrestling matches. For the first time in his life, Woody had a best friend. When he heard late in 1929 that his mother had

Woody *(left)* and Matt Jennings *(right)* shared a love of old-time country music.

Woody learned country songs and guitar-picking techniques by listening to the Carter Family. *Left to right:* Maybelle, A. P., and Sara Carter.

died, it was as though "somewhere on the outskirts of town, a high whining fire whistle seemed to be blowing." Woody felt close enough to Matt to tell him about his sad family history.

Like Woody, Matt loved music. The two friends listened to old-time country bands on radio shows such as *The Grand Ole Opry,* broadcast from Nashville, Tennessee. Inspired by the rousing fiddle, guitar, and banjo music they loved, Matt and Woody practiced their own instruments. They learned foot-stomping country tunes like "The Virginia Reel" and "Old Joe Clark." Woody particularly liked the guitar picking of Maybelle Carter, who played with the Carter Family, a popular country band. He worked hard to copy her style. The boys spent most of their free time at Uncle Jeff's—Matt screeching away on the fiddle and Woody bumbling along on his guitar.

When he wasn't practicing his music, Woody visited the library, reading books on nearly every subject. He had no steady job, but by that time there was little work for anyone. The Great Depression had hit the United States in late 1929. Farmers, unable to pay their bills, lost their land. Banks and businesses struggled and closed. With no job and little money to begin with, Woody was scarcely affected by the depression. As the years passed, he simply kept strumming his guitar and haunting the library. Then adventure called.

For years, the Guthrie family had been talking about the lost silver mine of Charley's father, Jeremiah P. Guthrie. Legend said that "Jerry P." had found a rich vein of silver in the Chisos Mountains of southern Texas. He had marked the spot with a piece of paper wired to a rock, drawn a crude map of the location, and never returned.

Uncle Jeff believed the tale. When someone suggested a trip to search for the mine, he eagerly agreed. Woody's brother Roy had recently moved to Pampa. He wanted to go along. Woody naturally favored any kind of adventure. Charley, now married to a large, pinched-faced fortune-teller named Bettie Jean, was eager to get away. He signed up for the trip, too.

The four men packed an old Model T truck. Under a canvas stretched across the truck bed, they stuffed musical instruments, beans and corn whiskey, shovels and pickaxes, gasoline—and Woody.

For two days the men traveled, first west to Amarillo, then south, stopping only to fill the tank with gasoline or change a flat tire. Woody spent most of the trip strumming his guitar and watching the country change from wheat fields to cotton fields to grazing land to desert. In northern Texas, wind was king, Woody decided as he watched tumbleweeds roll freely across the plains. In southern Texas, cactus and mesquite ruled. Finally, the

Woody discovered peace and splendor in the beautiful Chisos Mountains of Texas.

Chisos Mountains rose on the purple-pink horizon, the first real mountains Woody had ever seen.

When they reached their destination, the men soon realized they would never find the lost mine among the craggy canyons and rocks. But they stayed anyway, enjoying the peace and beauty of the area. "The feel and the breath of the air was all different," said Woody, "new, high, clear, clean, and light."

They spent nights in an abandoned adobe house, making music and eating beans. After a week, the four Guthrie men headed home. But the light, the colors, the sights, and the sheer power of the place stayed in Woody's memory, awakening his soul to the immensity of his country and to the beauty of his world.

Dust storms hit the Great Plains in the 1930s, smothering crops and ruining homes.

4

"Dust Can't Kill Me"

The depression still held the country in its clenched fist. Even the back-to-work programs of Franklin D. Roosevelt, elected president in 1932, provided little relief. And gradually the oil around Pampa ran out. Then, across the American plains, the rain stopped falling and the land was gripped with drought.

Still aimless, without a steady job, Woody continued practicing guitar with Matt Jennings. Eventually, they played well enough to team up with another guitar player, Cluster Baker. The three called themselves the Corncob Trio. At their first gig, a dance at a roller-skating rink, they earned five dollars. Job offers didn't come

From left to right: Matt, Woody, and Cluster Baker formed the Corncob Trio around 1931.

rolling in, though, so mostly they played at each other's house parties.

The Jennings house became a favorite spot for weekend get-togethers. With an audience watching, Woody, now twenty years old, told jokes, mimed to music, and made faces. He often made up rhymes and played with words, turning "New York" into "Yew Nork," for instance. He did anything to be the center of attention.

Matt's sister, fifteen-year-old Mary Jennings, took notice of Woody's "cornball" act. She recognized the qualities that made Woody different from other young men. Before long, Mary seemed special to Woody, too. Soon they were going to movies and working together on jokes, gossip, and stories that Woody sometimes printed

in little homemade newspapers. A few months later,
Woody asked Mary to marry him.

Though surprised at the proposal, Mary decided that
having Woody for a husband might make life interesting.
She told him yes. But her father said no. Not only was
Mary too young, but Woody wasn't Catholic like the
Jennings family was—and he didn't have a job.

Woody didn't give up. He continued courting Mary,
while she tried to convince her mother that theirs was a
good match. Finally, Mrs. Jennings signed the consent
form allowing her underage daughter to get married. On
October 28, 1933, with no family present, Woody, twenty-
one, and Mary, sixteen, became husband and wife.

The newlyweds moved into an apartment above Uncle
Jeff. Soon after, Jeff found jobs for Woody, Mary, himself, and his wife, Allene, with a new traveling show,
planned and paid for by a rich rancher named Claude
Taylor. They all spent the winter at Taylor's ranch rehearsing the show—a mixture of music, jokes, dancing,
and magic tricks. Dressed in a beard and wig, Woody
acted the part of an old farmer. He also played his guitar
and told jokes between numbers.

Taylor wasn't experienced in show business, however.
The show opened in the spring of 1934 but lasted only a
few performances. The best things Woody and Mary
gained from the experience were a honeymoon of sorts at
Taylor's ranch and an old typewriter that Taylor gave
Woody when the show closed.

Back in Pampa, Woody and Mary moved into a rickety
shack. Woody's life was full and fascinating. He worked

on and off at the drugstore. He read about subjects that lured him, including adobe houses, the law, and the occult. He pounded out stories on his typewriter. He earned money from sign painting and also painted pictures of his wife, Jesus, Abraham Lincoln, and others. He considered becoming an artist for a while. Filled with clever, creative ideas, he sent advertising slogans and cartoons to large companies. The companies sent him job offers, money, and free products in return. He accepted the money and the products, but not the jobs.

Woody even started his own fortune-telling business. He claimed he fell into the job by accident when a man appeared at his home looking for Bettie Jean, his father's fortune-telling wife. Woody printed up business cards that read "Divine Healing and Consultation." During the year he practiced fortune-telling, his services were in great demand. His success came from listening carefully while his customers talked, then using his common sense to help them solve their worries.

Music still took up much of Woody's time, however. After years of practice, the Corncob Trio was becoming popular, playing at saloons, barn dances, and sometimes on the radio. Woody also performed with Uncle Jeff at rodeos, carnivals, parades, and fairs. "It was along in these days I commenced singing," Woody wrote. "I guess it was singing," he added, poking fun at his plain, nasal voice.

Around 1935, Woody typed up a songbook called `Alonzo M. Zilch's Own Collection of Original Songs and Ballads.` Some of the songs were traditional ballads. Others were Woody's words set to old melodies. Throughout his career, Woody frequently wrote new lyrics for old songs, often using tunes performed by the Carter Family. Writing down new tunes would have been difficult anyway, because Woody couldn't read or write musical notes.

With the little he earned, Woody bought only what he needed at the moment, then gave away the rest of his money. His casual attitude toward finances began to annoy his friends and family. Mary worried about money, too—especially in the spring of 1935, when she told Woody she was pregnant. And there was another worry on everyone's mind that spring.

Across the Great Plains, from Canada to Texas, the terrible drought continued. Fields dried and crops died. Wind lifted the soil and blew it across the land in roiling black clouds. Dust seeped into houses and settled on furniture, dishes, and food. People walked in dust, breathed dust, and ate dust. On April 14, 1935, the great dust storm blew into Pampa.

The black cloud stretched from east to west across the horizon as it rolled toward town, with winds gusting to seventy miles an hour. People dashed into their houses and stuffed rags and towels into the cracks around the windows and doors. They covered their mouths and noses with wet washcloths. Many thought the end of the world had arrived.

When the storm hit, Woody and Mary's house became so dark that they could barely see the walls around them. The lightbulb in the living room looked like a

A dust storm hits a small town in Kansas, in April 1935, turning the sky black.

tiny glowing ember. The storm raged until after dark. The next morning, Woody looked out at a different world, a world he eventually described in a song called "Dust Storm Disaster."

Discouraged, many people in Oklahoma, Texas, and other Great Plains states gave up trying to wrestle a living from the parched earth. They packed and moved, leaving behind their homes and friends. Notices sent by California fruit growers promised jobs in "the Golden State." So people traveled west, where they hoped life would be better. They sang "California Blues," made famous by country singer and yodeler Jimmie Rodgers. In California, Rodgers sang, the water tasted like cherry wine, and the weather was so fine that you could sleep outside every night.

Despite the dust and drought, Woody and Mary stayed in Pampa. But Woody felt that the town had nothing more to offer him. He had played at all the dances, read all the books, and painted all the signs. Even his father was gone—he had left Bettie Jean and moved to Arkansas.

November 1935 brought the birth of Gwendolyn Gail Guthrie, called "Teeny." In honor of his daughter's

Country star Jimmie Rodgers sang about the good life in California.

Families from Oklahoma and other Dust Bowl states traveled by car to California, hoping to find work.

arrival, Woody composed "Curly-Headed Baby," which he crooned to her like a lullaby. He had been excited about the idea of having a baby. But when his daughter arrived, reality arrived with her. The responsibilities of fatherhood made Woody feel uneasy and trapped.

He watched the stream of travelers heading for California. He watched the dust sweep across the dead fields. Sometimes he followed the dust, taking short trips out of town—to East Texas, to Oklahoma, to Arkansas to visit Charley. When he showed up at home, he fidgeted, slept, or fought with Mary. He let his hair grow wild, and he rarely bathed.

For years Woody had soaked up knowledge. Now it was all boiling inside him like a kettle with a plugged spout. The trips helped him work off some of his boredom, some of his extra energy. He learned new songs as he traveled. He wrote new songs about the dust and the promised land of California. Some of the songs were funny, some mocking, some full of rebellion. One song, titled "Dusty Old Dust" but usually called "So Long, It's Been Good to Know Yuh," told of a storm that covered the land with dust and blocked out the sun.

As the months passed, Woody began drifting farther and farther from Pampa. He hitched rides and sneaked onto moving freight trains. To earn money, he sang in bars and restaurants. He slept in smelly flophouses, in alleys, on the desert sand, and in rocking boxcars. But he always came home to Mary—until his restlessness boiled up again. Then, sometime in 1936, twenty-four-year-old Woody packed his paintbrushes and his guitar and drifted west toward California.

Unemployed people poured into California. Many, like these men in Los Angeles, were sent back out of the state by train.

5

"Hard Travelin'"

Woody rode the rails most of the way to California. It was an illegal and dangerous way to travel. If riders got caught, railroad security men might beat them or send them to jail. On crowded boxcars, ruffians often started fights.

At towns along the tracks, Woody earned his way by painting signs and posters and playing his guitar in saloons. If no jobs were available, he begged at private homes. Once Woody didn't eat for two days. Another time he traded his only sweater for a plate of beans. But the situation looked brighter when Woody finally reached California. "The world turned into such a thick green garden of fruits and vegetables that I didn't know if I was dreaming or not," he wrote.

But the beauty existed only in the scenery. Since the depression had started, more than half a million desperate people, including entire families, had come to California looking for work. Finding camps of hungry, unemployed people, Woody learned that the promise of good jobs in California had been a lie. With four to ten workers competing for every one job, planters could hire fruit and vegetable pickers at starvation wages. Even families lucky enough to get work could not survive on the pay.

Sitting around campfires at night, Woody heard talk about rich and poor, about workers and bosses, about labor unions trying to fight for workers' rights. He learned

Migrant fruit pickers lived in tents and shacks, usually in camps with no toilets, running water, or health care.

how longtime Californians bullied the migrants flooding into their state, scornfully calling them "Okies" since many of them came from Oklahoma. Hungry and cold himself, Woody wended his way north to Turlock, a town in central California. He visited an aunt there, then headed home to Pampa.

Woody felt angry about the hopeless lives of the migrant workers. But he turned this anger into humor. He wrote parodies, songs that poked fun at serious problems, setting the words to the country tunes the migrants knew and loved. One song, `Do Re Mi,` told about illegal roadblocks the Los Angeles police set up at the California border. The police refused entry to out-of-state travelers who didn't have jobs or enough "do re mi" (money) to live on:

Oh, if you ain't got the do re mi, folks,
If you ain't got the DO RE MI,
Why, you better go back to beautiful Texas,
Oklahoma, Kansas, Georgia, Tennessee.
California is a garden of Eden,
A paradise to live in or see,
But believe it or not
you won't find it so hot,
if you ain't got the do re mi.

Woody made a number of trips between California and Texas in 1936 and 1937, but Pampa seemed dull compared to the Golden State. Late in 1936, Mary was pregnant again. But by spring 1937, Woody was gone, hitchhiking back to California. He promised Mary that he'd send for her and the children when he was settled.

By then, a number of Guthries had migrated to Glendale, near Los Angeles, including the aunt whom Woody had visited in Turlock. He moved in with her, then began to pal around with a cousin named Jack Guthrie. Jack, a skilled guitarist and a fine singer, called himself "Oklahoma." He appeared in singing contests, rodeos, and cowboy shows wearing fancy Western outfits. Jack began taking his scrawny, scruffy cousin along as his "hillbilly" sidekick. As soon as Woody tilted his head back, pointed his chin, and began to sing, people took the waif into their hearts.

In July 1937, the two Guthries began their own half-hour radio show, *The Oklahoma and Woody Show*, broadcast at 8 A.M. daily on KFVD in Los Angeles. They received no pay. The cowboy music they performed wasn't Woody's favorite, but Jack did most of the singing and yodeling, leaving Woody to play his guitar and harmonica. Fan mail poured in. Soon the station asked them to do a second half hour at 11:00 P.M. They still were unpaid, but the publicity was excellent.

After a month, Woody invited a friend named Maxine Crissman to sing with him on the show. Woody described Maxine as a tall thin-faced farm girl with a rough, husky voice. He called her "Lefty Lou." Like Woody, Maxine loved singing old hymns and ballads. Together, their voices blended with stunning harmony.

In September, Jack quit the show. To keep the show going, Woody invited Maxine to join him as cohost.

Between the ballads, hymns, and hillbilly tunes that Woody and Maxine preferred to sing, they chatted and read letters from fans. Woody told tales, using his "country hick" voice to share his "Cornpone Philosophy." "I guess I didn't git so much in my head," he would say, "but I've had less headaches a gittin by on an empty one." Sometimes he talked for as long as fifteen minutes at a time.

Most listeners were farm families who had fled the dust in the drought land. They loved the show. Woody and Lefty Lou were country people, too, singing about the listeners' lives. Fan letters poured in, nearly five

In 1937 radio listeners in Los Angeles tuned in to hear Woody *(second from left)* and his cousin Jack "Oklahoma" Guthrie *(right)*. Maxine Crissman *(left)* joined Woody as cohost when Jack left the show.

hundred in September and more than fifteen hundred in November.

One letter wasn't complimentary, however. While on the air, Woody had casually used an offensive term refer-ring to black people. When he received a critical letter from an African American college student, Woody imme-diately apologized over the radio. He promised never to use the word again, then tore all the pages containing the offensive word out of his personal songbooks.

Fans began requesting their own copies of the songs Woody and Maxine sang, so they printed a songbook called Old Time Hill Billy Songs. On each page, Woody added jokes and comments, such as "Lefty Lou typed off a lot of theese songs and I tyyped off a bunCh. YoU WOnt HavE any Troubbel tellxng whech ones I rote."

When KFVD gave Woody and Maxine another show, this one at noon, Woody began singing his own composi-tions and writing new songs for the show. One day, when asked where he was from, Woody replied that he came from the Oklahoma hills. Pleased with the way the words sounded, Woody wrote his classic "Oklahoma Hills" in time for that evening's show. He wrote the chorus in minutes.

On clear nights, the radio signal carried Woody's pro-gram all the way to Pampa. Mary Guthrie, now twenty, listened proudly. Woody was finally becoming a success. Perhaps now he would send for her, the way he had promised. When Frank Burke, the station's owner,

Maxine Crissman ("Lefty Lou") and Woody pose with a sign for their radio show in 1937.

finally began to pay Woody and Maxine for their shows, Woody did send for Mary, Gwen, and four-month-old Sue—the daughter he had never seen. The family moved in with relatives until they could find their own place.

Life in California wasn't as wonderful as Mary had hoped, however. Living with strangers felt awkward. Wrapped up in preparing and performing his radio show, Woody didn't spend much time with her and the children. Then his old habits appeared—staying out late or not coming home at all.

By the end of 1937, Woody and Maxine were earning sixty-five dollars a week—more than twice as much as factory workers earned in those days. Then a radio station in Tijuana, Mexico, with a signal so powerful it could reach a wide area of the United States, offered to hire Woody and Maxine for seventy-five dollars a week. The station, XELO, also wanted Woody to gather a group of country performers for a nightly three-hour broadcast.

Woody's relatives had clamored to be on his show. Recently, Uncle Jeff, Allene, and Mary's brother Matt had all arrived from Pampa. Woody could hire them all. He broke his contract with KFVD and hauled the performers to Tijuana. As master of ceremonies, Woody organized the XELO show and introduced the performers. Often, however, he spent too much time drinking in the local bar to give clear direction, so the show was chaotic. After a few weeks, the station stopped paying them. Less than a month after they trooped to Mexico, Woody and the crew returned to Los Angeles. KFVD gave Woody and Maxine back their morning and noontime radio shows.

Stung by his experience at XELO, Woody turned down new radio offers, including decent ones from national country music shows. He also refused offers from companies that wanted to advertise on his show. He took pleasure in offending them. Opportunities slipped away.

Woody's relationship with Mary was slipping away, too. The family moved into their own apartment in May 1938, along with Woody's younger brother, George, who had just arrived in California. Woody continued to be distant, sometimes completely ignoring his unhappy wife.

In June 1938, Woody and Maxine asked Frank Burke for a break. Maxine felt ill and exhausted. Woody didn't seem to care much about the show anymore. On June 18, Woody and Lefty Lou gave their last performance together on KFVD.

Burke had another offer ready, though. In addition to running KFVD, Burke was active in labor unions and the Democratic Party. He published a small political newspaper called *The Light*. Burke knew that Woody had a good connection with working people. Would Woody visit the migrant camps and investigate conditions there? Rumors abounded that workers who supported labor unions were being beaten and jailed. Would Woody check into that? Burke explained that Woody's investigation would help the campaign of Culbert Olsen, the Democratic candidate for governor of California. The report would also run in Burke's newspaper.

Within days, Woody hopped a boxcar and began rolling north. Arriving in central California farm country, Woody soon realized that conditions had changed little in the year since he had last visited the migrant camps. He found families settled wherever they could, living in shelters built from scraps and cardboard. Drinking water often came from filthy streams that were also used as toilets. Children suffered from sores, worms, and lice and sometimes died of starvation and disease. Often, fruit-laden trees grew within sight of the workers' hovels—but armed guards protected the trees.

When they found jobs, entire families worked, sometimes earning as little as three dollars a week picking crops. Union organizers encouraged the migrants to stand up against the growers and demand decent wages,

Police watch cotton strikers in Tulare County, California. Strikes often led to violence and bloodshed between strikers and the authorities.

even go on strike if necessary. But when the growers learned of these efforts, they hired local bullies called vigilantes to break up picket lines, attack union support-ers, and demolish migrant camps. The police sided with the growers and the vigilantes.

Despite their suffering, the migrants, many from Okla-homa and Texas, welcomed Woody into their tents and shacks. They shared their meager food and offered him a bed. In return, "harsh voiced and nasal, his guitar hang-ing like a tire iron on a rusty rim," he sang—songs that spoke to the migrants of the land and homes they had left behind, of the miseries life had delivered to them.

Shocked by conditions in the camps, Woody vented his anger by writing political songs. "Dust Bowl Refugees" tells of fleeing the "dust bowl" only to die in the "peach bowl." "Dust Pneumonia Blues" pokes fun at Jimmie Rodgers, whose "California Blues" had inspired so many people to head west. In "Dust Can't Kill Me," simple, three-line verses describe how drought and dust destroyed a man's family, home, and wheat—only to have him stubbornly vow each time, "But it can't kill me, Lord. It can't kill me."

After a few months, Woody returned to Los Angeles. Calling himself "Woody, the Lone Wolf," he went back on the air with a half-hour radio program. But he also continued to visit migrant camps and dash out of town to sing for striking workers.

Around this time, Woody wrote "I Ain't Got No Home in This World Anymore," an angry response to a Carter Family song, "This World Is Not My Home," which was popular in the camps at the time. The Carters' song encourages people to accept the sorrows of this world and meekly await the joys of heaven. Woody's song, set to the same tune, reveals the pointless suffering of people in an uncaring world. It tells of the rich man taking the farmer's home and driving him out, the banker taking his crops, and the farmer's wife dying. It speaks of gathering the rich man's corn and working his mines only to learn:

This wild and wicked world
Is a funny place to be.
The gambling man is rich
and the working man is poor
And I ain't got no home in this world anymore.

Ever since he began traveling, Woody had been an observer. With `"I Ain't Got No Home,"` he was ready to act. He began voicing his growing political views on his radio show.

In the 1930s, some people in the labor movement supported communism, a form of government that was practiced in the Soviet Union at the time. Communists called for the end of capitalism—private ownership of business and property. They believed that all people in a country should own everything in common. Many Americans, however, saw communism as a threat to democracy. They attacked communists as "left wing" troublemakers.

To Woody, the communists looked like the only ones fighting for workers' rights. Most of the union organizers Woody met in the migrant camps belonged to the Communist Party. Woody liked anyone willing to help "his" people, even radical groups such as the communists. Once, when asked if he had any objections to communism, Woody replied, "Left wing, right wing, chicken wing—it's the same thing to me."

At KFVD, Woody met a man named Ed Robbin. He hosted a political radio show and also wrote for a communist newspaper, *People's World.* Robbin invited Woody to sing at a local Communist Party rally, and Woody received a thunderous ovation there. Soon he was performing regularly at party gatherings. His background and his scruffy appearance worked to his advantage with left-wing audiences. He looked oppressed— like the migrant workers he sang about. Woody had never cleaned up or dressed to impress anyone. Now that his audiences liked him that way, he acted even more countrified.

Ed Robbin thought Woody was an uneducated hick. So Robbin was surprised when Woody began publishing cartoons and a short, sly political column called "Woody Sez" in *People's World.* The column and cartoons poked fun at current events. Filled with misspelled words and poor grammar, the pieces also maintained Woody's country bumpkin image.

Woody continued writing songs, including ballads about well-known outlaws such as the Dalton Gang, Belle Starr, and Pretty Boy Floyd. Even in these songs, Woody managed a few digs at an uncaring society that forced thousands of people into homelessness and poverty. An outlaw, said Woody in "The Ballad of Pretty Boy Floyd," wouldn't rob you with a fountain pen or drive a family from its home the way a banker would.

In July 1939, Woody met the respected actor Will Geer. Although not a member of the Communist Party, Geer believed in the union cause. He was planning to tour migrant camps and put on skits that showed the advantages of unions. He liked touring with a ballad singer, so he asked Woody to go along. While preparing for their tour, Will took Woody to entertain at Hollywood parties, including one for writer John Steinbeck. Steinbeck had just published a novel called *The Grapes of Wrath* about the plight of migrant workers.

Will, tall and imposing, and Woody, tiny and fragile looking, worked well together. By then, Woody had improved as a performer. When he talked or told jokes in his Oklahoma drawl, his timing was perfect. When he sang, every word was sharp and clear. His voice—which he said sounded like "ash cans in the early morning"—pierced listeners' hearts.

While Will and Woody toured the migrant camps, war loomed in Europe. Adolf Hitler's fascist government had come to power in Germany and now threatened neighboring countries. The communist Soviet Union had made a pact with Germany, agreeing to remain neutral if Germany attacked another country. The pact upset many communists in the United States and made communism even more unpopular with the American public. But Woody wasn't very concerned with political shenanigans on the other side of the world. He still performed at Communist Party functions and promoted the party on his radio show.

After the tour ended, Woody and Will continued visiting migrant camps on weekends. Woody's frequent absences were hard on Mary. Expecting their third child, she worried that Woody wasn't saving any money for the new baby. KFVD was paying Woody one dollar a day for his radio show, only enough to cover carfare. His only other income came from appearances at political events and in saloons.

One weekend in October, while Woody sang at a rally for cotton strikers, Mary gave birth to Will Rogers Guthrie, named after an American humorist whom Woody admired.

Though proud that Woody was in demand as an entertainer, Mary worried about his communist leanings. She was also disappointed with his neglect of her and the children. Frank Burke was disappointed in Woody, too. His support of the communists was causing problems at Burke's radio station. Woody's audience drifted away.

Around the same time, Will Geer left for New York to star in a Broadway show, and Woody began performing on his own again. But the communist crowd had grown weary of his routine, and Woody didn't fit in with Will's Hollywood crowd.

That autumn, Woody wrote a song called "I'm A-Goin' Back to th' Farm." A short time later, his radio show ended for good. In November 1939, Woody packed up the family and headed home to Pampa.

Woody, Mary, and their three children *(from left to right)*, Gwen, Sue, and Will Rogers

6

"Ramblin' Round"

The Guthries moved back into the same old Pampa shack. But instead of welcoming Woody home, people in town snubbed him. Some were disgusted with his communist politics. Others, mostly friends and family, resented the way he treated Mary. For Woody, life in Pampa was unbearable.

Woody quickly hit the road. In January 1940, he hitched rides to New York City, where he stayed with Will Geer, his wife, Herta, and their new baby. Woody spent his days wandering the city of 7.5 million people, soaking in its sights: the subway, skid row, panhandlers, rich ladies in their furs, ethnic neighborhoods, gangsters, Wall Street, Times Square, the new Rockefeller Center. Woody felt most at home in the bars where the seamen swaggered and boasted. But the twenty-seven-year-old also seemed like an innocent child in the bustling city. He was amazed when he learned how much the Geers paid to rent their apartment: one hundred fifty dollars a month, not a year.

Woody kept odd hours, and he didn't like to take baths. He was an unpleasant houseguest, and Herta Geer quickly became fed up with him. So Woody moved in with Burl Ives, a folksinger he had met in California, then to a room in a cheap hotel. There, on February 23, 1940, musical history was made.

The song "God Bless America," written by Irving Berlin, had haunted Woody as he hitched across the country. It seemed to blast at him from every car radio, every jukebox. The patriotic song was popular with most Americans, but Woody hated it. The song made it seem as though people weren't important to the country. In his shabby hotel room, Woody decided to write a song to counter Berlin's, to let people know that America and its beauty belonged to them. "This land is your land, this land is my land," wrote Woody:

```
From California to the Staten Island,
From the Redwood Forest, to the Gulf
stream waters,
God blessed America for me.
```

Woody made many changes before the verses he called "God Blessed America" satisfied him. Some years later, Woody renamed the song "This Land Is

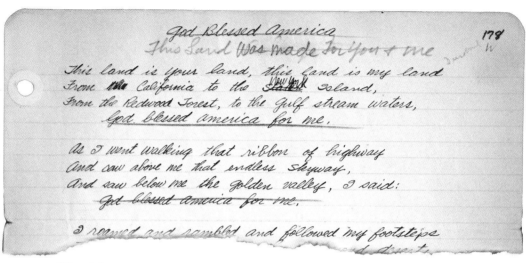

God Blessed America 178

This Land Was made for You + me

This land is your land, this land is my land
From the California to the New York island,
From the Redwood Forest, to the gulf stream waters,
God blessed america for me.

As I went walking that ribbon of highway
And saw above me that endless skyway,
And saw below me the golden valley, I said:
God blessed america for me.

I roamed and rambled and followed my footsteps

Woody's handwritten lyrics to "God Blessed America," later renamed "This Land Is Your Land," show some of the revisions the song underwent.

Your Land." But for a long time after he created it, Woody forgot about the song.

On March 3, Woody joined Will Geer and some other folksingers at New York's Forrest Theater for a concert to benefit farmworkers. After greeting the crowd, Woody launched into his dust bowl songs. Then he charmed the audience with tales of his misadventures as a greenhorn in New York. He said that when he got off the overcrowded subways, he kept finding strange shoes on his feet.

One of the other performers at the concert, Alan Lomax, was assistant director of the Archive of Folk Song at the Library of Congress in Washington, D.C. For years, Lomax had traveled the country with his father, John, recording the music and stories of the American people— songs such as "Home on the Range" and "John Henry."

Lomax was riveted with excitement when he heard Woody sing. Here was a man singing the old traditional songs in the old traditional way. Yet many of Woody's songs had an added twist—they were political.

By the end of the month, Woody was sitting in a Washington recording studio with Alan Lomax. Woody sang, strummed his guitar, blew his harmonica, told jokes, and talked about his life and travels. Lomax recorded every word of the casual three-day session for the Library of Congress.

In April Lomax arranged for Woody to perform on a CBS radio program called *Columbia School of the Air.* Woody received two hundred dollars in pay, a lot of money for a single performance. Later that month, CBS paid him fifty dollars to sing "Do Re Mi" on a program called *The Pursuit of Happiness.*

Woody's biggest break came when Lomax arranged for Victor Records to produce two vinyl record albums of Woody's dust bowl ballads. On May 3, Woody stood before a microphone in Victor's studio, guitar slung over his shoulder. He sang song after song, including "So Long, It's Been Good to Know Yuh," which he hadn't sung since his Pampa days. Victor paid him three hundred dollars for the session.

During his time in New York, Woody had been writing Mary and sending her money. With the Victor albums completed, the time had come to visit her and the children. Instead of riding the rails, however, Woody drove to Texas in his own new Plymouth. He stopped in Washington, D.C., on the way, long enough to write

Woody's radio jobs earned him more money than he'd ever had before.

introductions for each protest song in Alan Lomax's new songbook, *Hard-Hitting Songs for Hard Hit People.*

He also picked up a traveling companion in Washington—a tall stringy twenty-year-old named Pete Seeger. Seeger, the son of a wealthy left-wing family, loved folk music and was learning to play the banjo. He had been in the audience at the Forrest Theater and had met Woody through Alan Lomax. He hoped to learn everything he could about folk music from Woody.

On the road to Pampa, Woody and Pete spent a night in Oklahoma City, where they performed for some strikers and unemployed workers. Afterward, Woody wrote the song "Union Maid," set to the tune of "Pretty Red Wing":

There once was a **union maid** who never was afraid
of **goons** and ginks and company finks
and the deputy sheriffs who made the raids;
She went to the union hall when a meeting it
was called,
And when the company **boys came** 'round
she always stood her ground.
Oh, you can't scare me, I'm sticking to the union.
I'm sticking to the union, I'm sticking to the union.
Oh, you can't **scare me,** I'm sticking to the union.
I'm sticking to the union till the day **I die.**

"Union Maid" would be Woody's most popular song for the next ten years.

Arriving in Pampa, Woody soon learned that little there had changed. After Mary's mother begged Pete to make Woody treat Mary better, Pete scampered west. Woody spent a few more days with his family, then bounced out of their lives again, heading back to New York.

Victor released Woody's *Dust Bowl Ballads* in July 1940, but the records sold few copies, most in left-wing circles. Woody returned to singing at communist gatherings and in bars and nightclubs. Gilbert "Cisco" Houston, a singer Woody had met in California, arrived in New York and joined Woody in some of his club acts. Gradually, Cisco became Woody's closest friend.

In New York, Woody met the country's most famous folk-singers, including Huddie "Leadbelly" Ledbetter.

One of the greatest influences in Woody's life at this time was Huddie Ledbetter, known as Leadbelly. Leadbelly played twelve-string guitar and sang in a deep, husky voice. Woody had probably heard some of Leadbelly's most famous songs—"Irene," "Midnight Special," and "Pick a Bale of Cotton"—before he ever met their creator. Although they had shared the stage at the Forrest Theater, Leadbelly and Woody seemed to have little in common. Leadbelly was a huge African American man who had been in prison for murder. He was twenty-five years older than Woody. But the two men shared a love of music. And during their time together, Leadbelly taught Woody not only about music but also about life.

In August Woody sang "So Long, It's Been Good to Know Yuh" on the first performance of

Alan Lomax's radio show *Back Where I Come From.* A few days later, he signed a contract to sing regularly on the show for one hundred fifty dollars a week. Other radio offers followed. CBS asked Woody to host a weekly show called *Pipe Smoking Time.* That job paid two hundred dollars a week, giving Woody a total weekly salary of three hundred fifty dollars at a time when the average workingman made twenty-six dollars a week. In less than a year, Woody had hit the big time.

He still supported the Communist Party, although he had never officially joined the group. He still wrote `"Woody Sez,"` which now ran in the *Daily Worker,* another communist newspaper. He still performed at Communist Party functions. But Americans, particularly business leaders, had become very suspicious of communism by then.

Radio stations relied on sponsors—businesses that paid to run their commercials during the shows. Woody knew that his shows' sponsors wouldn't approve of his beliefs and many of his political songs. If the sponsors withdrew their commercials, Woody's shows would be canceled. He knew he had to change his focus or give up the shows and the money. But he truly believed his music was good for the United States. If he didn't believe that, he told Alan Lomax, he would shut his mouth and catch the first train out of the country.

Woody had a difficult choice to make. He wanted to stick by his beliefs. But he liked making enough money to support his family. Compromising somewhat, he decided to quit writing `"Woody Sez"` and to continue with the radio shows.

After *Pipe Smoking Time* opened on November 25, 1940, Woody immediately sent for his family. Mary and the kids arrived in New York by train, and they all moved into a four-room furnished apartment near Central Park. For the first time, Mary had extra money to spend. There were nannies, nights out, and parties at home. The children loved eating frost out of the refrigerator's freezer and flushing the toilet—luxuries the family had never been able to afford in Texas.

As the host of *Pipe Smoking Time,* Woody opened the show, told stories, sang songs, and introduced other performers. But the show's producers allowed Woody no artistic freedom. He followed a written script. He couldn't ad-lib, tell his own stories or jokes, or sing what he wanted. He couldn't use his sly humor to spice up the act. His song "So Long" was even turned into a commercial for the tobacco company sponsoring the show.

No one had ever told Woody what to do before. Now he was doing as he was told: singing songs merely to entertain, not to teach people. Woody tolerated his new success for a while. After all, he was earning more money than he had ever earned in his life. But then, once again, he began boiling like a kettle with a plugged spout. Only this time, instead of bubbling with pure energy, he bubbled with resentment and disgust.

As the year rolled over into January 1941, Woody disappeared for several days. When he came home, he told Mary to start packing. The Guthries were getting out of New York. They loaded as much as they could into the car, then headed south. In El Paso, Texas, where Mary's brother Matt now lived, Woody left the family for a few days. He wanted to visit the Chisos Mountains again, hoping the desert peace would seep into his soul and renew his spirit.

The Guthries were soon on the road once more, this time west to California. Woody settled the family in a shabby hotel in Columbia, a mountain town in the central part of the state. Once a booming gold rush town, Columbia now boasted mostly ghosts and memories. There, Woody earned some money singing in the local saloons.

Realizing that Woody was a talented writer with interesting stories to tell, Alan Lomax had suggested that Woody write his autobiography. So in Columbia, Woody spent most of his time in the hotel room, clacking away on a typewriter. After two weeks, Woody realized he couldn't raise his children on only fresh mountain air. The family headed for Los Angeles. Woody hoped that Frank Burke would give him back his old radio show at KFVD.

Woody noticed changes as they traveled south through California. Germany had invaded Poland in September 1939, beginning World War II in Europe. Although the United States did not enter the war at first, American factories began producing weapons and equipment for the Allies—the nations fighting the Germans. In California, Woody saw that many Okies had found work in the thriving defense plants. The migrant camps Woody had once visited were only memories.

Woody's job at KFVD was only a memory, too. Frank Burke didn't want him back. Woody began to regret fleeing New York. Perhaps they should return, he thought. He contacted the producer of *Back Where I Come From* and asked for his old job back. But the show had been canceled.

The Guthries were stuck in Los Angeles with no money and no work. On February 27, 1941, Woody wrote in the back of an old songbook, "Everything looks like it's all bogged down. But we'll pull through. Always do."

With most of his time free, Woody rediscovered the library and began reading again. He also wrote endlessly, not his autobiography as Alan Lomax had suggested, but ramblings and word play. He wrote even with the children crawling across his lap. For the first time, Woody was really getting to know Gwen, Sue, and Will, spending time with them, making up silly songs and games.

Back in Los Angeles in 1941, Woody put on a few shows, but money soon ran short.

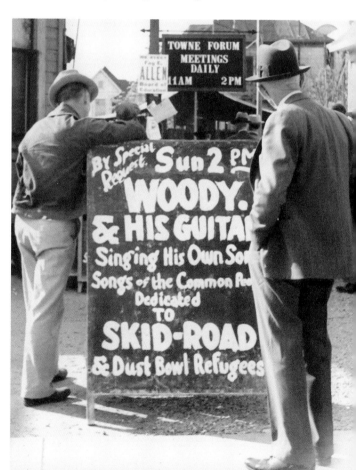

Construction of the Grand Coulee Dam inspired Woody to write some of his greatest songs.

Through an acquaintance in Los Angeles, Woody met a film director who was planning to make a documentary movie about the Grand Coulee Dam on the Columbia River in Oregon. The director needed someone to narrate the film, and he interviewed Woody for the part. In early May 1941, desperate and not yet knowing if he would be hired, Woody loaded the family into the car and headed for Portland, Oregon.

When Woody arrived at the dam headquarters, he learned that the movie deal had fallen through. But seeing the hungry, travel-weary family, their belongings spilling from their battered car, the head of the dam project took pity on them. Learning that Woody was a musician, the project director offered him $266.66 to spend thirty days writing songs about the dam.

For the next month, Woody visited sites on the river, scribbling ideas in notebooks, talking to workers, and watching them pour their sweat into the dam. The dam was a U.S. government project that would bring electricity to rural areas and provide jobs to the people who lived nearby. Many of those people were Okies who hadn't yet found steady work. It pleased Woody that the dam was a government project. Helping people and giving them jobs was exactly what he felt a government should do.

He had written few songs since he left New York, but as the concrete dam grew, Woody's creative dam burst. In twenty-eight days he wrote at least twenty-six songs. "Roll On, Columbia" and "Grand Coulee Dam" describe the splendor of the river and its dam. "Hard Travelin'" and "Jackhammer John" honor the men who did the work. "Pastures of Plenty," set to a traditional tune, honors the migrants who had been pushed from their homes and their lands:

I've worked in your orchards of peaches and prunes,
Slept on the ground in the light of your moon,
On the edge of your city you've seen us and then,
We come with the dust and we go with the wind.

Shortly after Woody's month on the dam ended, a letter arrived from Pete Seeger in New York. Seeger and some other folksingers had formed a group called the Almanac Singers. They were planning a tour to help organize labor unions and support strikers across the country. Could Woody join them? Leaving Mary and the children in Portland to fend for themselves, Woody once again breezed out of their lives.

pastures of plenty
this train is bound for glory
"Deportee" ("Plane W

Woody plays guitar, while Pete Seeger picks the banjo.

7

"All Work Together"

Woody rode a cattle car east and arrived in New York in time to record two albums, *Sea Shanteys* and *Sodbuster Ballads,* with the Almanac Singers. On July 4, 1941, Woody and three other members of the Almanac Singers—Pete Seeger, Lee Hays, and Millard Lampell—opened the tour in Philadelphia, Pennsylvania. (Other singers joined the group at different times over the years.)

That summer in union halls across the country, the four young men roused tough, tired, and rowdy workers to their feet and singing for the union. Woody, now twenty-nine, felt fulfilled by the work. Simply by writing songs

The Almanac Singers helped make folk music popular in the United States. In this 1941 performance, Woody is on the far left. Pete Seeger is third from right.

and singing them, he and the Almanac Singers were helping change workers' lives.

As the Almanacs drove from city to city, Woody and Lee Hays played word games. Woody often got the giggles creating mixed-up words and turning names such as Herbert Hoover into "Hoobert Heever," "Heebert Hoover," and "Hovert Heeber." By August, the group had driven and sung its way to Los Angeles.

In September Mary arrived in Los Angeles from Portland. She was sick of being dumped in strange towns with three children while Woody wandered the country.

Gwen was old enough to start school—the family needed roots. Mary knew that Woody believed in his work, but she didn't like Woody's new friends or his communist way of thinking. She wanted Woody to settle down and become a dependable husband and father.

Woody asked Mary to return to New York with him but warned her not to count on him settling down. It was clear to Mary that Woody wasn't going to change. Taking the children, she returned to her family in Texas. It would be a few years before Woody and Mary divorced, but their marriage was essentially over.

Lee Hays and Millard Lampell had headed back to New York separately, leaving Woody and Pete Seeger on the West Coast. Before returning to New York, Woody and Pete detoured through Seattle, where they sang at a fund-raising party on September 20. The locals called the party a "hootenanny." Woody loved the word. Back in New York, at a house where some of the Almanac Singers lived, the group gave Sunday afternoon concerts and called them hootenannies. Musicians of any race or musical style were welcome to play there. Audiences were free to sing along.

Meanwhile, Woody continued to write. Words gushed from his typewriter, pen, and pencil stubs: journal entries, new songs, revisions of old songs, his rambling autobiography, a newsletter called *The Daily Almanac*. He threw some of his writing away. What he didn't toss out, he pitched into his "filing cabinet"—a large trunk in his room at the Almanac House.

That fall of 1941, the Almanac Singers performed as many as six shows a night. They gave additional free performances in subway stations—their favorite places to play. There, among the people, Woody did his finest work. Onstage, though, Woody didn't always behave. Sometimes he gave a noble performance. But if the audience members didn't pay attention, Woody might make up insulting verses about them or simply walk out. Sometimes he drank too much and fell asleep during shows.

By this time, World War II raged in both Europe and Asia. Japan, which had signed a pact with Germany, was invading other Asian and Pacific countries. On December 7, 1941, Japan attacked Pearl Harbor in Hawaii, bringing the United States into the war.

Because the Almanac Singers had left-wing views, some people had called them un-American. But when the nation entered World War II, the group proved that they were just as patriotic as anyone. They began to sing war songs such as "Round and Round Hitler's Grave," a song that attacked the German dictator. Woody quickly wrote new war verses to go with his old songs.

Their change in focus put the Almanacs in demand everywhere. They even auditioned at the Rainbow Room, a nightclub on the top floor of Rockefeller Center—the classiest joint Woody had ever seen. As soon as he arrived, Woody knew he didn't belong there. When the show's producers began discussing what kind of makeup and costumes the Almanacs should wear, the rest of the singers knew it, too. They hustled out the door.

The Almanac Singers reached their widest audience on Valentine's Day 1942. They sang on a radio program

Woody met his second wife, Marjorie, in 1942.

called *This Is War,* broadcast over all the national radio networks. But a few days later, New York newspapers began revealing the Almanacs' ties to the Communist Party and its newspapers. Bookings vanished. Only the Sunday hootenannies remained to provide income.

But the lack of work didn't bother Woody very much—because by early 1942, he was falling in love. While rehearsing for a show of dances set to poetry and folk songs, Woody had met a twenty-five-year-old dancer named Marjorie Greenblatt Mazia.

The couple felt a spark immediately, but one gigantic problem loomed. Marjorie was already married, although unhappily, to a man who lived in Delaware. Woody was married, too, but he and Mary planned to divorce. So did Marjorie and her husband, although neither couple's divorce would become final for several years.

In the spring of 1942, Woody moved into Marjorie's New York apartment. The move was for practical as well as romantic reasons. The publisher E. P. Dutton had given Woody a five-hundred-dollar advance to finish his autobiography, which he called "Boomchasers." Woody needed a quiet place to complete the book. Since Marjorie was leaving for a national tour with the Martha Graham Dance Company, her apartment would be empty.

Woody stayed on when Marjorie returned. She soon learned that he hadn't done much work on the book, though. Take it seriously, she urged—writing was his job now. Woody followed her advice, although he still performed occasionally with the Almanac Singers. He also wrote new war songs, such as `Talking Hitler's Head Off Blues.` On his guitar he painted a slogan: "This Machine Kills Fascists." This slogan expressed Woody's belief that music was powerful and could move people to take action against evil leaders like Hitler.

In June 1942, Marjorie learned she was pregnant. Both she and Woody were excited, and Woody started drawing cartoons about the child, a boy he nicknamed Railroad Pete. He also started a journal for Pete, telling the unborn baby his deepest thoughts and dreams. In September

Woody wrote about one of his worst fears—that he wasn't entirely sane. One minute he felt nervous and afraid, the next minute big and strong.

Hoping to keep her pregnancy private, Marjorie moved back to Delaware to await the baby's birth. She gave up her New York apartment, so Woody moved in with some Almanac Singers. He spent his days and nights singing in saloons with his old friend Cisco Houston, working on his autobiography, and writing letters to Marjorie. Upset by Marjorie's absence, he sometimes threw tantrums when he saw her, then wrote to apologize. Red devils with pitchforks were poking around in him, making him say cruel things, he explained.

Woody *(left)* and Cisco Houston *(right)*, 1944

By December 1942, the Almanac Singers had disbanded. Members had moved away, gotten new jobs, or joined the army. Woody found another apartment and decided to start his own group, called Woody Guthrie's Headline Singers. The group included harmonica player Sonny Terry, guitarist Brownie McGhee, and Leadbelly—all African Americans.

At the time, African Americans were often forbidden to mix with white people at schools, hotels, restaurants, and other public places. In Baltimore, Maryland, after playing onstage with Woody, McGhee and Terry were led to a separate dining table for black people. Not even allowed to join them, Woody became furious. Quietly, he told his two partners to leave the room. Then, before he followed, he calmly walked over to a table loaded with food and up-ended it. He would no longer tolerate prejudice as he once had in Los Angeles.

On February 6, 1943, Woody's imaginary Railroad Pete vanished when Marjorie gave birth to a daughter, Cathy Ann Guthrie. At the hospital, Woody studied the baby through the nursery room window. Then he went home and wrote a seventy-page poem describing how he felt. Mostly, he wrote, he wanted to hold Cathy. He wanted to listen to her "GUGGLE AND GOOGLE AND GURGLE AND GEEGLE AND SQUEAK AND SPEAK AND TALK."

Cathy Ann's arrival coincided with the release of Woody's autobiography, renamed *Bound for Glory*. Mary, his three oldest children, and the Almanac Singers were never mentioned in the book, which made it as much fiction as nonfiction. The reviews, however, praised Woody's writing, calling him a natural poet and a national treasure.

Thirty-year-old Woody Guthrie was back in the big time. His Headline Singers were successful. His publisher wanted him to write a second book. He won a seventeen-hundred-dollar fellowship to write more books and songs. *Life* magazine printed his photograph. He performed again on national radio.

Then, Uncle Sam came calling.

Rather than join the army, Woody signed on as a merchant marine during World War II.

8

"Over the Waves
and Gone Again"

With the war persisting in Europe and the Pacific, the United States needed more troops, even thirty-year-old men with crooked elbows like Woody. In May 1943, he received notice to report to the army.

For months Cisco Houston had been nagging Woody to join him in the merchant marine, a fleet of civilian ships that carried supplies and troops to the war zones. Because the work was vital to the war effort, merchant marines didn't have to serve in the army.

When his draft notice arrived, Woody finally allowed Cisco to drag him down to the National Maritime Union to sign up for the merchant marine. He and Cisco shipped

Woody in his merchant marine uniform, 1945

out in late June on the *William B. Travis,* part of a convoy, or group of ships, bound for Europe. Being "on the road" again thrilled Woody, even if the road was a rolling ocean patrolled by enemy submarines. Finally, Woody was doing more to lick Hitler than simply writing songs.

Woody started on the ship as a dishwasher, then served meals to some navy men onboard. Like a merry leprechaun, he soon worked his way into the men's hearts and became the ship's good-luck charm. The other merchant marines shook their heads at the sight of Woody's bunk covered with books, a typewriter, papers, and musical instruments. Signs everywhere warned the men not to keep journals—not to write down anything about where they were going or what they were doing. That information could help the enemy if the ship were captured. Yet Woody constantly scribbled in his little notebooks, recording events, thoughts, and conversations.

Early in the voyage, Woody began building what he called a "wind machine," perhaps to distract the men from the dangers lurking in the water around them. On the railing near the stern of the *Travis*, Woody made the device from old wooden crates, rubber bands, and other scraps. The wind machine spun and sang in the breeze as gears whirled, propellers twirled, and feathers whirred. At sunset, the crew gathered near the machine. Then, depending on the gang's mood, Woody and Cisco would sing sad, sweet, lively, or rude songs, while Woody's wind machine added a comforting harmony of its own.

One night, the *Travis* survived a submarine attack, although some of the other ships in the convoy were destroyed. Afterward, Woody, Cisco, and their friend Jimmy Longhi talked about life and death. Woody shared the story of his family's troubles, then revealed a private fear: "I'm pretty sure I've got the same thing my mother had . . . I just feel *queer* sometimes."

In November, Woody came home on leave. Marjorie had rented an apartment on Mermaid Avenue in Brooklyn, one block from the beach at Coney Island, a popular summertime amusement park. Woody spent his days there wandering the beach with baby Cathy in her stroller, past the carousel horses halted mid-stride, the boarded-up souvenir shops and hot dog stands.

Woody, Cisco, and Jimmy Longhi shipped out again in January 1944. Their new ship, the *William Floyd,* was bound for North Africa. Arriving at a port in Algeria, Woody saw horrifying poverty. He and the crew sorted through their leftovers, giving the best scraps of food to families onshore. The Algerians were Muslims who valued cleanliness as much as food, so Woody collected soap and hauled it in pillowcases to the town center. He sang for the children there, while their mothers gratefully accepted his gift.

Home again in March, Woody heard that the Asch Record Company wanted to record some real American folk music. Uninvited, Woody appeared at the office of the owner, Moses Asch. "I'm Woody Guthrie,"

Left to right: Jimmy Longhi, Cisco, and Woody saw the world while on duty in the Merchant Marine. (The woman with whom they are standing is unidentified.)

he announced, hunkering down on Asch's floor. "I want to make some records."

Beginning on April 16, 1944, Woody—joined off and on by Cisco Houston, Sonny Terry, Leadbelly, and Alan Lomax's sister, Bess—recorded one hundred thirty-two songs for Asch. During the last session, Woody threw in "This Land Is Your Land," possibly the first time he had sung it since writing it in his New York hotel room four years earlier.

Woody and his friends put to sea again that summer, on a ship called the *Sea Porpoise*, which was carrying three thousand soldiers to Europe. On June 6, 1944, while the *Sea Porpoise* was still crossing the Atlantic, the Allies attacked the beaches of Normandy, France, beginning the invasion of Europe. Hoping to halt the arrival of more enemy troops, German submarines patrolled the ocean relentlessly.

Frightened of enemy attacks, Jimmy Longhi wanted to stay above deck, near the *Sea Porpoise*'s lifeboats. Woody, however, insisted that Jimmy and Cisco go with him to entertain the soldiers deep in the bowels of the ship. For hours, while bombs exploded around the ship, the trio organized dances and sang to the frightened men.

In July, the soldiers dropped over the side of the ship to join the invasion in France, leaving the merchant marines behind. Woody, Jimmy, and Cisco were sitting in their cabin talking when, suddenly, Woody sailed toward the ceiling, and Jimmy's bunk crashed to the floor. The sound of bursting metal rang through the ship. An underwater mine had exploded beneath the *Sea Porpoise*.

Woody and Cisco dashed up on deck, only to realize that Jimmy hadn't followed. With water flooding into the ship, they raced back to their cabin and hauled their unconscious friend to safety. Somehow, the helpless ship stayed afloat. Another boat towed it to England. Woody and the other merchant marines then sailed for home on a troop ship, arriving in time for the presidential election of 1944.

President Franklin D. Roosevelt, a Democrat, was running for a fourth term in office against Republican Thomas Dewey. In late September 1944, Woody joined the Roosevelt Bandwagon, a group of left-wing entertainers planning a multistate tour on Roosevelt's behalf. The Bandwagon didn't contribute much to the president's cause, however. Newspapers scorned the performers, calling them communists and singling out Woody as an

Woody (holding guitar) poses with the Roosevelt Bandwagon, 1944.

irresponsible hobo. At the first show, someone even lobbed stink bombs into the crowd.

In December, back in New York with Marjorie, Woody began a fifteen-minute radio show on WNEW. He chose "This Land Is Your Land" for his theme song and quickly printed a songbook called *Ten Songs for Two Bits* to go with the show. During his opening broadcast, Woody described his outlook on music:

> I hate a song that makes you think you're not any good. I hate a song that makes you think you are just born to lose. Bound to lose. No good to nobody. No good for nothing. Because you are either too old or too young or too fat or too slim or too ugly or too this or too that. . . . Songs that run you down or songs that poke fun of you on account of your bad luck or your hard traveling.
>
> I am out to fight those kinds of songs to my very last breath of air and my last drop of blood.
>
> I am out to sing songs that will prove to you that this is your world and that if it has hit you pretty hard and knocked you for a dozen loops, no matter how hard it's run you down nor rolled over you, no matter what color, what size you are, how you are built, I am out to sing the songs that make you take pride in yourself and your work.

Woody's words endured. The radio show didn't, ending after only a few months.

In March 1945, Moses Asch released six of Woody's

songs on records, but there was little public interest in them. That same month, the army again came looking for Woody. He was inducted on May 7, 1945—the same day Germany surrendered to the Allies.

The war in Europe was over, but Woody was sent to basic training in Texas. Now thirty-two, he was older than the other recruits and so small that no uniform fit him. On the obstacle course, he fell into puddles and off fences. In June, Mary and their three children, whom Woody hadn't seen for four years, visited him at the base in Texas. By this time, Woody and Mary's divorce was final, and Mary told Woody that she was planning to re-marry. Woody felt relieved and sad at the same time.

In early June, Woody was sent to Scott Field, near Al-ton, Illinois, to attend army Teletype school. He was cer-tain he would be discharged any day, especially after Japan surrendered to the Allies in August. But no dis-charge came, and Woody grew downhearted. He spent his free time writing—short stories, war ballads, letters to friends and to Marjorie. The letters became sad and con-fusing, and the word *nervous* appeared often. Woody's mood worsened when he heard Jack Guthrie, his cousin from California, sing `"Oklahoma Hills"` on the jukebox. Jack was getting credit for creating Woody's song.

In an October letter to Marjorie, Woody confessed that he felt strange: "It seems like a hundred pound sack of frogs and snakes are tied to each of my arms, my mouth is full of rabbit hair and my brain is caught in a net it can't get out of." He cheered up a bit when Marjorie's divorce at last became final. During a two-week leave in November, he and Marjorie were married in New York's City Hall. Then Woody moved on to a new assignment at an air base near Las Vegas, Nevada.

He kept writing letters. Sometimes they stretched to forty or fifty pages of tiny, tight handwriting. Often, his thoughts seemed to get stuck. On December 19, 1945, he wrote to Marjorie, "Just dizzy. Woozy. Blubberdy. And scrubberdy and rustlety, tastlety, I was saying. Fantiffy, fantiffy, fantoy, fantoy. Poodle de doodle de dum dum. Doodle doodle dum." Then the letter continued in a normal way.

The next day, Woody's discharge came through, and he went home to Marjorie.

From a Ferris wheel, two women view Coney Island crawling with vaca-
tioners. After World War II, Americans wanted to enjoy the peace and
prosperity of their country.

9

"Why, Oh Why?"

Woody was home again at Mermaid Avenue. A few days after he arrived in New York, he joined a new singing group called People's Songs. Started by Pete Seeger, the group hoped to hold hootenannies and write protest songs for unions. But People's Songs had a big problem: Americans didn't want to hear any more protest songs.

The nation had come through hard times—the Great Depression and World War II—into a period of prosperity and peace. Americans wanted to enjoy the good times. They didn't want left-wingers demanding change. What's more, relations between the capitalist United States and the communist Soviet Union had begun to grow frosty. Communism became more unpopular than ever in the United States. To many

Americans, People's Songs seemed more of a menace than a benefit.

The group wasn't in great demand, but Woody soon discovered a substitute audience, one that delighted him much more—three-year-old Cathy, whom he called "Stackabones" and "Stacky." Woody spent a good part of his days watching Cathy grow. Together, Woody and Cathy played records, sang, and danced. He painted the walls of her bedroom with flowers and wrote about her in his journals. Every little thing Cathy did or said became inspiration for a song, from "Wake Up" time until "Sleep Eye" time. Nothing was too silly or too ordinary to put to music:

```
Take my brush,
Take my broom,
Clean and I clean
around my room,
Clean and I clean
around my room
To make it pretty and shinyo.
```

He also wrote songs about Cathy's endless questions and his patient, but silly, answers:

```
Why can't a bird eat an elephant?
Why, oh why, oh why?
'Cause an elephant's got a pretty hard
skin.
Goodbye, goodbye, goodbye.
```

Moses Asch recorded two albums of Woody's songs for

Woody began to write songs for children after the birth of his daughter Cathy.

ongs to Grow On and _Work Songs to Grow_
ld better than any of his other records. To
songs had a purpose—to bring families to-
In a booklet accompanying one album,
nts to watch their children and copy their

'ing other songs around this time, but
le one was "The Ballad of
d." Based on a real incident, the
nan blinded by police after he uses
or whites. Words still poured out
writer—mostly articles, poems, letters,

and journal entries. But work on his second book, *Ship Story*—about his experiences in the merchant marine—didn't go well.

Despite the joy he took in Cathy, Woody's home life had problems. Woody and Marjorie adored each other, but there was also much to quarrel about: Woody's sullen moods, the lack of money and Woody's habit of giving it away, his drinking, and his habit of vanishing when Marjorie needed him to watch Cathy.

Woody's behavior in public was also becoming more and more unusual. During performances, he sometimes endlessly repeated verses or sang rude songs to shock the audience. He missed punch lines, forgot lyrics, seemed confused, and stumbled at times. When driving, Woody deliberately broke the law, running red lights and driving the wrong way on one-way streets.

Yet life had many joys. The tiny three-room apartment on Mermaid Avenue was filled with music, books, and company. The house became a refuge for kids from troubled neighborhood families. Aspiring teenage musicians appeared, hoping to play a few chords with the legendary Woody Guthrie. He gladly obliged, often jamming with them for hours.

The year 1947 began happily for Woody. He had set aside *Ship Story* and begun work on a new novel. The first chapter was going well. Marjorie was expecting a baby brother or sister for Cathy, who turned four on February 6. On February 9, Woody performed for some electrical workers in New Jersey—a rare treat, since it was a union crowd.

Woody arrived home late that evening and, to his dismay, smelled smoke and ashes. A note stuck to the door told him to go to Coney Island Hospital at once. There, Woody's dreaded fears were confirmed. He learned that Marjorie had rushed out of the house for five minutes to buy some oranges that afternoon. She had left Cathy sitting on the sofa, listening to the radio. Somehow the wires on the radio had ignited, setting the sofa and Cathy on fire. Minutes before Marjorie returned, a neighbor had rushed in and wrapped Cathy in a blanket to smother the flames.

Like Woody's sister and father, Cathy had been badly burned. Her skin seared, Cathy cried throughout most of the afternoon. When her father arrived at the hospital, however, she was singing, much the same way Woody's sister Clara had chatted cheerfully on her deathbed. The next morning, Cathy died.

Woody endured many painful losses in his life, including the death of Cathy.

Afterward, Cisco Houston and Jimmy Longhi took Woody for a walk on the beach. Suddenly, Woody flung himself on his back on the sand, kicked his arms and legs wildly in the air, and howled. Then he stood up, shook off the sand, and walked home.

He later wrote, "Cathy sang and danced right up to the last, and we know that she would like for her Mommy and her Daddy to feel this same way. So, let's not feel low and lonely like we might like to feel, but let's feel high and mighty like Cathy would ask us to feel."

But part of Woody died with his daughter, and he didn't feel high and mighty. He found it hard to concentrate, hard to settle. Marjorie, too, was feeling sad and alone. She imagined she saw Cathy and heard her crying and calling for her mother.

In mid-May, while touring in the West, Woody wrote Marjorie, "Your old man is in hard shape. I don't know what has hit me. I've never felt this low before. . . . All scrabbled up." Woody canceled his bookings and headed home. He drank less, stayed home more, and settled down to write a new novel, "Study Butte," about the journey to the Chisos Mountains to search for Jerry P. Guthrie's silver mine.

By the summer of 1947, life seemed brighter again. Gwen Guthrie, Woody's eleven-year-old daughter, came from Texas to visit. On July 10, a son, Arlo Davy, was born. Woody also received a big check from a record company. After learning that Woody, not Jack Guthrie, had written "Oklahoma Hills," the company cleared up the mistake and sent Woody nearly twelve hundred dollars in royalty payments, a portion of the profits from the record sales.

In 1948, at age thirty-six, Woody heard that a plane full of migrant workers had crashed, killing all on board. The workers were all Mexicans who had been deported—sent back to Mexico after harvesting crops in California. The song Woody wrote in response, `"Deportees"` (also called `"Plane Wreck at Los Gatos"`), asks:

```
Is this the best way we can grow our big
orchards?
Is this the best way we can grow our good
fruit?
To fall like dry leaves to rot on my topsoil
And be called by no name except deportees?

Good-bye to my Juan, good-bye Rosalita,
Adios mis amigos, Jésus y Maria;
You won't have your names when you ride the
big airplane,
All they will call you will be deportees.
```

Although Woody was writing as many songs as ever, singing opportunities were becoming scarce. After the war, the government began searching out people who were considered disloyal to the United States. Their names appeared on a blacklist, and many entertainers, writers, educators, government workers, and others— especially people involved with the Communist Party— were listed. Often, those listed were fired from their jobs

and couldn't find other work. Because of their communist ties, the members of People's Songs were likely
candidates for the blacklist. Bookings disappeared. The
group folded early in 1949.

In autumn of that year, a publisher turned down an 842-
page version of "Study Butte" (after Woody's death, the
book was published as *Seeds of Man*). Soon afterward, in
December, Woody's friend Leadbelly died. With this
blow, Woody again lost his drive. His writing seemed
tired and repetitive. He began drinking more and acting
in bizarre ways. He spoke in long confusing sentences,
and his speech slurred. Once, he even threatened Marjorie
with a kitchen knife.

And even though he spent time playing and singing
with them, Woody wasn't as patient or as loving with his
children as he had been with Cathy. By then there were
two boys: two-year-old Arlo and one-year-old Joady Ben.
When daughter Nora Lee arrived in the fall of 1950, the
apartment on Mermaid Avenue bulged with children. The
family moved to a roomy apartment near Coney Island
Hospital. There was only one problem—they couldn't afford it. Then Pete Seeger rode to the rescue by recording
one of Woody's songs.

With the collapse of People's Songs, Seeger had started
a new group called the Weavers. The group became popular by avoiding communist functions and adapting folk
songs, such as Leadbelly's "Irene," to make them more
commercial. Soon the Weavers were at the top of the pop
music charts, thanks in part to Woody's `"So Long,`
`It's Been Good to Know Yuh."`

Woody plays with *(from left to right)* Nora, Joady, and Arlo at Coney Island in 1951.

Woody had hated turning that song into a commercial for a tobacco company ten years earlier. This time, he removed all mention of dust and changed it into a love song for the Weavers. Decca Records gave Woody a ten-thousand-dollar advance for the song. He would also receive almost a penny for every record sold and three cents for every copy of sheet music sold.

Now the Guthries could afford the new apartment. They paid off their debts, bought a new car, and had enough left over for Marjorie to open her own dancing school. Woody's other problems remained, though. He lurched when he walked and never bathed at all. He seldom performed and wrote little. Even his handwriting looked different—his tidy, tight script ballooned, oozing over lines and margins. He wrote with colored pens and pencils, sometimes making each word or each letter a different color.

His words made little sense, and his love of word games spewed out of control. He even played with his name, writing it as "WWWW Gee Gee Gee Gee," "WWGeehawker," "Goody Wuthrie," "Woodridge Duthridge," and "Woodvine Twiner." He signed his name on everything, as though to prove to himself that he still existed.

Marjorie and many of Woody's friends thought that drinking had ruined his brain. Although Marjorie still loved her husband, his odd behavior frightened her. She never knew when he would be in an ugly temper and do something terrible. She worried that he would hurt the children. When Woody began to wander the country again, Marjorie encouraged his trips. His absence meant life would be peaceful for a time.

Woody traveled by bus, hitched, and rode the rails. Usually, he headed west to California, visiting friends and relatives along the way. But people didn't welcome Woody as before. He was no longer a merry, traveling troubadour with fascinating tales to tell and songs to sing. He looked more like a shabby, smelly tramp who needed a bath and a haircut.

By 1952 Marjorie had decided to divorce Woody. She asked him to move out for good. He began sleeping on friends' sofas, in doorways, and in cheap hotel rooms. He spent his time writing Marjorie, asking her to forgive him and promising to stop drinking if she let him come home. Sometimes he terrorized the family with unexpected visits.

During the summer of 1952, Woody was in and out of hospitals. Although one doctor thought Woody might be suffering from a mental illness called schizophrenia, Woody blamed alcohol for his problems. But Marjorie wondered if something else might be the cause. In July, she convinced Woody, then forty years old, to check into Brooklyn State Hospital. A doctor there described Woody as withdrawn and fidgety, his movements and speech jerky. He grimaced and sniffed. His face showed no expression, except an occasional smile.

Even in the hospital, Woody continued to write, and he noted on September 20, "I wonder if it could be chorea?" Sometime in the next two days, the doctors confirmed Woody's worst fears: He was suffering from Huntington's chorea, or Huntington's disease. The disease affects the central nervous system. The nerves lose their ability to function, and victims gradually lose control of their bodies and often their minds. Huntington's is hereditary—it can be passed down from parents to children. There is no known cure.

For years, Woody had suspected that he had his mother's disease. Once he knew the truth, he couldn't accept it. In a letter asking the hospital to discharge him, Woody insisted he was an alcoholic experiencing withdrawal. But he also wrote that he was going to research and write about Huntington's disease. Then he left the hospital and looked for a place to hide.

pastures of plenty
this train is bound for glory
"Deportee" ("Plane W

Woody's health began to decline in the 1950s, just as folk music surged in popularity.

dust can't kill me
Dust Pneumonia Blues
The Ballad o
Goin' Back to th' Farm

10

"So Long, It's Been Good to Know Yuh"

In September 1952, Woody left Brooklyn State Hospital, hoping to get back together with Marjorie. But she refused. So he headed for California once more. Will Geer, Pete Seeger, and Cisco Houston were already there, trying to escape the blacklist. Woody moved into a cabin on Will and Herta Geer's property in Topanga Canyon, a rugged, secluded area north of Los Angeles. Many blacklisted refugees lived there. They welcomed Woody as the grand old man of folk music. His symptoms from Huntington's had come on so gradually, few noticed he had changed.

Besides, once in California, the disease retreated. Woody's thoughts seemed clearer and sharper. He performed in local hootenannies and started writing songs again. He also discovered he loved working with clay on a potter's wheel.

While working in the potter's shed, he met a young woman named Anneke Marshall. Fascinated by Woody, the twenty-year-old invited him to live with her and her new husband. After a month, Woody, then age forty, announced that he had fallen in love with Anneke. She decided she was in love with Woody, too. Two days later, she left her husband and ran off with Woody. They ended up in Florida, where they moved into an abandoned bus on the edge of a swamp.

Woody Guthrie and Anneke Marshall, 1953

Never having known Woody when he was well, Anneke thought his jerks and stutters were just Woody. It isn't clear if she knew he had Huntington's. If she did, she must not have realized how serious the disease is or that it could be passed on to his children. By June 1953, she was pregnant. Living in conditions unfit for a baby, the couple pondered what to do.

They returned to Topanga Canyon in July, and Woody surrendered to despair. By the end of the year, he scarcely spoke. Nevertheless, he and Anneke were married in December 1953. Thinking a return to New York might help Woody, the couple headed east. They settled in a dreary apartment. Woody spent his days listening to his old albums again and again and again.

Anneke delivered a girl, Lorina Lynn, on February 22, 1954. Drinking and delirious, Woody never went to the hospital to see Anneke and the baby. But he managed to gather enough energy to clean the apartment and cover the walls with merry cartoons to welcome his new daughter home.

The baby inspired Woody for a time. He wrote plays and tried performing with his friends. In Florida, he had reinjured his right arm, so his guitar playing was painful to hear. But no one had the heart to tell him.

That summer Woody fled west again. He hitched rides and rode the rails, visiting places from his past: California, Oregon, Washington, Colorado. He went to Texas to visit Mary, his children, and his old friend Matt Jennings. The trip was Woody's personal farewell to his country. When he returned to New York that fall, he checked himself back into Brooklyn State Hospital. Two months later, in a poem, Woody wrote:

```
Huntington's Chorea
Means there's no help known
In the science of medicine
For me . . .
Maybe Jesus can think
Up a cure of some kind.
```

Reading continuously as though to shut out the world, Woody now turned to the Bible. Reassured by its message, Woody finally faced his illness. In December, in a letter to his father, who was then living in Oklahoma City, Woody admitted that he had Huntington's.

Sometimes Woody's mind was steady enough to write letters and an occasional song. Most of the time, however, his words were nearly impossible to decipher. He wrote "NINETEENE   HUNDRITDTHE   &   DOUBLEDY FIVE" to indicate the year 1955.

Early in 1956, concerned friends formed the Guthrie Children's Trust Fund, an organization that would promote Woody's works and collect the royalties for his children. At that time, royalties were few, so the group staged a fund-raising concert at Pythian Hall in New York. This was the concert where forty-three-year-old Woody struggled to his feet and raised his fist in a silent salute.

Soon after, Anneke allowed Lorina Lynn to be adopted by another couple, and she filed for divorce. Marjorie, although remarried by then, quickly resumed her familiar

By the late 1950s, Woody needed full-time medical care.

role as Woody's caretaker. Woody moved to Greystone Park, a hospital in New Jersey. He wrote fewer letters. One was signed, "`Lovey Me.   Writey   me. Savey me.   Lordey God, Woody.`"

Woody's creative years ended as his beloved folk music exploded on the popular music scene. The time was right for protest songs. As the communist scare faded in the late 1950s, people became more politically active. The Civil Rights movement—the fight to win equal rights

Bob Dylan, shown here in the early 1960s, revered Woody Guthrie and even traveled to Greystone Park Hospital to sing for him.

for African Americans—gained momentum. Pete Seeger visited college campuses, showing students how to use music to denounce injustice. Popular groups such as the Kingston Trio and the Brothers Four sang Woody's songs.

A college student named Robert Zimmerman showed up at Greystone in January 1961 to play guitar and sing for his idol, Woody Guthrie. The student had curly hair like Woody's and held his guitar the same way. A year later, Zimmerman's song "Blowin' in the Wind" made him one of the most famous singers in the United States. By then he was known as Bob Dylan.

Later in 1961, Woody moved back to Brooklyn State Hospital. He was closer to Marjorie there, and she could take him to her home for visits. Around this time, Woody's son Arlo, by then a teenager and hoping to become a performer in his own right, learned all the verses to "This Land Is Your Land," including a defiant one:

As I went walking, I saw a sign there,
And on the sign it said "No Trespassing."
But on the other side it didn't say nothing,
That side was made for you and me.

By 1965 Woody could no longer walk. He communicated by blinking his eyes. But Marjorie believed that inside Woody's crumbling body, his mind was clear. He moved to the Creedmoor State Hospital in Queens, New York, in 1966. By then he was little more than a sack of bones. That autumn, he heard a recording of nineteen-year-old Arlo singing "Alice's Restaurant," a song that pokes fun at government and the police. A friend thought Woody smiled as he listened.

Woody Guthrie died on October 3, 1967, at the age of fifty-five. His body was cremated, then the ashes were delivered to Marjorie and the children. Together, Marjorie, Arlo, Joady, and Nora visited Woody's favorite beach in Coney Island, intending to pour Woody's ashes into the ocean. But the ashes wouldn't pour out of the holes that Marjorie had punched in the lid of the can. So Arlo hurled the can into the water, and together they watched it sink beneath the waves.

pastures of plenty
this train is bound for glory
"Deportee" ("Plane W

Pete Seeger *(on banjo)*, Arlo Guthrie *(behind Seeger)*, Bruce Springsteen
(far right), and other folk and rock artists pay tribute to Woody in
September 1996.

dust can't kill me
Dust Pneumonia Blues
The Ballad
A Goin' Back to th' Farm

"Born to Win"

"My dad's journey was a spiritual journey," Arlo Guthrie once said, "it was a mystical journey his whole life." Even after death, Woody's spiritual journey continued.

In 1988 he was inducted into the Rock and Roll Hall of Fame. *Woody's 20 Grow Big Songs,* an unpublished songbook lost for forty years, was released with a cassette in 1992. In September 1993, Pampa, Texas, held its first annual Woody Day celebration. In September 1996, the new Rock and Roll Hall of Fame and Museum in Cleveland, Ohio, sponsored a ten-day tribute to Woody. The finale of the festivities was a concert of Woody's words and music. In 1999 an exhibition celebrating Woody's life began touring the country.

"I ain't a writer," Woody wrote in the early 1940s. "I want that understood. I'm just a little one-cylinder guitar picker." But Woody Guthrie was a guitar picker *and* a writer. He was also a poet, artist, prophet, vagabond, philosopher, and an imperfect genius—brilliant, but flawed.

Because of his flaws, many people respected Woody's talent, but disliked the man. "I don't know that anybody admired the person," said Arthur Stern, Woody's fellow Almanac Singer. "He was offensive. He was insulting. [But] the artist was incredible, so I think everybody put up with the personality for the diamonds that came out of that mind and mouth."

Above all, Woody will be remembered for his music— for his guitar, which "buzzes and rumbles and bounces and skitters and sings all at the same time," and for his voice, which Arthur Stern compared to the slender, pointed blade of a stiletto. It "went right in," Stern said, "pierced you through and through, and your hair stood on end. It was a scream or a sneer of extraordinary power."

Years after his death, Woody's name still summons the image of a tiny man with a bushy head of hair, chin tilted toward the sky, eyes closed, fingers nimbly plucking the strings of a battered guitar, a man who found music all around him:

Music is in all of the sounds of nature and there never was a sound that was not music—the splash of an alligator, the rain dripping on dry leaves . . . a long and lonesome train whistling down . . . kids squawling along the streets—the silent wail of wind and sky. . . . Life is the sound and . . . the word is the music and the people are the song.

Woody Guthrie gave the world his music, and the people are still singing.

Music brought Woody Guthrie joy, and his songs brought more joy to millions of people.

Selected Bibliography

Guthrie, Woody. *Born to Win.* Ed. Robert Shelton. New York: Macmillan, 1965.

Guthrie, Woody. *Bound for Glory.* New York: Dutton, 1943.

Guthrie, Woody. *Pastures of Plenty: A Self Portrait.* Ed. Dave Marsh and Harold Leventhal. New York: HarperCollins, 1990.

Guthrie, Woody. *Woody Sez.* New York: Woody Guthrie Publications, 1975.

Klein, Joe. *Woody Guthrie: A Life.* New York: Knopf, 1980.

Low, Ann Marie. *Dust Bowl Diary.* Lincoln, NE: University of Nebraska Press, 1984.

Robbin, Ed. *Woody Guthrie and Me: An Intimate Reminiscence.* New York: Lancaster-Miller, 1980.

Rutland, Robert Allen. *A Boyhood in the Dust Bowl, 1926–1934.* Niwot, CO: University Press of Colorado, 1995.

Yates, Janelle. *Woody Guthrie: American Balladeer.* Staten Island, NY: Ward Hill Press, 1993.

Other Resources

Videos

Hard Travelin'. Wombat Film and Video, 1984.

Woody Guthrie. BBC Lionheart Television (Arena), 1988.

Printed Music Collections

Guthrie, Woody. *Woody Guthrie Songs.* New York: The Richmond Organization, 1992.

Guthrie, Woody, and Marjorie Mazia Guthrie. *Woody's 20 Grow Big Songs.* New York: HarperCollins, 1992.

Audio Recordings

Bragg, Billy, and Wilco. *Mermaid Avenue.* Elektra Records, 1998.

Bragg, Billy, and Wilco. *Mermaid Avenue, Vol. II.* Elektra Records, 2000.

Guthrie, Woody. *The Asch Recordings.* Smithsonian/Folkways, 2000.

Guthrie, Woody. *The Ballads of Sacco and Vanzetti.* Smithsonian/Folkways, 1996.

Guthrie, Woody. *Columbia River Collection.* Rounder, 1987.

Guthrie, Woody. *Dust Bowl Ballads.* Budda Records, 2000.

Guthrie, Woody. *Greatest Songs of Woody Guthrie.* Vanguard, 1972.

Guthrie, Woody. *Nursery Days.* Smithsonian/Folkways, 1992.

Guthrie, Woody. *Sings Folk Songs.* Smithsonian/Folkways, 1989.

Guthrie, Woody. *Songs to Grow on for Mother and Child.* Smithsonian/Folkways, 1991.

Guthrie, Woody. *Struggle.* Smithsonian/Folkways, 1990.

Guthrie, Woody. *This Land Is Your Land: The Asch Recordings, Vol. 1.* Smithsonian/Folkways, 1997.

Guthrie, Woody. *Woody Guthrie: Library of Congress Recordings.* 1964. Reissue, Rounder, 1988.

Guthrie, Woody, Arlo Guthrie, et al. *Woody's 20 Grow Big Songs.* Rising Son Records, Inc., 1992.

Various performers. *Daddy O Daddy: Rare Family Songs of Woody Guthrie.* Rounder Records, 2001.

Various performers. *Pastures of Plenty: An Austin Celebration of Woody Guthrie.* Dejadisc, 1993.

Various performers. *A Tribute to Woody Guthrie.* Warner Bros., 1976.

Additional Resources

Smithsonian Folkways: <http://www.si.edu/folkways/40100.htm>
Woody Guthrie Archives: <http://www.woodyguthrie.org>
Woody Guthrie Foundation, 250 West 57th Street, Suite 1218, New York, NY 10107, (212) 541-6230

Source Notes

11   Henrietta Yurchenco, *A Mighty Hard Road: The Woody Guthrie Story* (New York: McGraw-Hill, 1970), 23.

14   Woody Guthrie, *Pastures of Plenty* (New York: Harper Perennial, 1992), 177.

20   Woody Guthrie, *Bound for Glory* (New York: New American Library, 1970), 158.

28   Ibid., 173.

31   Woody Guthrie, *Seeds of Man: An Experience Lived and Dreamed* (New York: E. P. Dutton, 1976), 122.

36   Guthrie, *Pastures of Plenty*, 5.

43   Guthrie, *Bound for Glory*, 223.

45   "Do Re Mi." Words and music by Woody Guthrie. TRO—Copyright © 1961 (renewed), 1963 (renewed) Ludlow Music, Inc., New York, NY.

47   Guthrie, *Pastures of Plenty*, 21.

48   Joe Klein, *Woody Guthrie: A Life* (New York: Knopf, 1980), 96.

52   John Steinbeck as quoted by Klein, *Woody Guthrie: A Life*, p. 160.

53   "Dust Can't Kill Me." Words and music by Woody Guthrie. Copyright © 1961 (renewed), 1963 (renewed) Ludlow Music, Inc., New York.

53   "I Ain't Got No Home." Words and music by Woody Guthrie. TRO—Copyright © 1961 (renewed), 1964 (renewed) Ludlow Music, Inc., New York.

54   Edward Robbin, *Woody Guthrie and Me: An Intimate Reminiscence* (Berkeley, CA: Lancaster-Miller, 1979), 32.

56   Woody Guthrie, notes for *Bound for Glory*, Folkways record album 2481, 1961.

60   "This Land Is Your Land." Words and music by Woody Guthrie. TRO—Copyright © 1956 (renewed), 1958 (renewed), and 1970 Ludlow Music, Inc., New York.

64   "Union Maid." Words and music by Woody Guthrie. TRO—Copyright © 1961 (renewed), 1963 (renewed) Ludlow Music, Inc., New York.

69   Klein, *Woody Guthrie: A Life*, 179.

71   "Pastures of Plenty." Words and music by Woody Guthrie. TRO—Copyright © 1960 (renewed), 1963 (renewed) Ludlow Music, Inc., New York.

80   Klein, *Woody Guthrie: A Life*, 254.

85   Ibid., 269.

86–87   Ibid., 275.

89   Woody Guthrie, *Born to Win* (New York: Collier Books, 1967), 223.

90   Klein, *Woody Guthrie: A Life*, 300.

91   Ibid., 303.

94   "Pretty and Shinyo." Words and music by Woody Guthrie. TRO—Copyright © 1953 (renewed), 1963 (renewed) by Folkways Music Publishers, Inc., New York.

94   "Why, Oh Why?" Words and music by Woody Guthrie. TRO—Copyright © 1960 (renewed), 1972 (renewed) Ludlow Music, Inc., New York.

98   Guthrie, *Born to Win*, 206.

98   Klein, *Woody Guthrie: A Life*, 340.

99   "Deportees." Words by Woody Guthrie; Music by Martin Hoffman. TRO—Copyright © 1961 (renewed), 1963 (renewed) Ludlow Music, Inc., New York.

103   Klein, *Woody Guthrie: A Life*, 379.

108   Guthrie, *Born to Win*, 248.

109   Klein, *Woody Guthrie: A Life*, 413.

111   "This Land Is Your Land." Words and music by Woody Guthrie. TRO—Copyright © 1956 (renewed), 1958 (renewed), 1970, and 1972 Ludlow Music, Inc., New York.

113   *Woody Guthrie*, BBC Lionheart Television (Arena), 1988.

114   Guthrie, *Pastures of Plenty*, 60.

114   *Woody Guthrie*, BBC Lionheart Television (Arena), 1988.

114   Ibid.

114   Ibid.

114–15 Guthrie, *Pastures of Plenty*, 106.

Index

Photographs are reproduced through the courtesy of: Woody Guthrie Archives, pp. 8, 10, 13, 15, 16, 18, 21, 27, 34, 47, 49, 58, 61, 65, 69 (Seema Weatherwax), 72, 74, 77, 79, 84, 86, 88, 95, 97 (Sid Grossman), 101, 106, 109, 112 (Roger Mastroianni), 115; Independent Picture Service, p. 6; Library of Congress, pp. 12 (HABS OKLA 54-OKE V 1-2), 32 (LC-USF-34-18262-C), 40 (LC-USF-34-56051), 44 (LC-USF-34-018452-E); © Bettmann/Corbis, pp. 24, 52, 104; © Frank Driggs Collection/Archive Photos, pp. 28, 63; © Ansel Adams Publishing Rights Trust, p. 30; Franklin D. Roosevelt Library, p. 38 (NLR-PHOCO-A-48223-3719-33); The John Edwards Memorial Foundation, Inc., at the Folklore and Mythology Center, University of California, p. 39; © American Stock/Archive Photos, p. 42; © Corbis, p. 70; National Archives, p. 82 (NWDNS-44-PA-1149); Keystone/Archive, p. 92; Theatre Collection, Museum of the City of New York, p. 110.

Front cover portrait: © Bettmann/Corbis